A Beginner's Handbook to Traditional Native American Beadwork

By

James Byrne
(Illustrated by Teresa A. Byrne)

authorHOUSE™

1663 LIBERTY DRIVE, SUITE 200
BLOOMINGTON, INDIANA 47403
(800) 839-8640
WWW.AUTHORHOUSE.COM

First published by AuthorHouse 05/06/05

ISBN: 1-4208-9947-3 (e)
ISBN: 1-4208-9948-1(sc)

Library of Congress Control Number: 2004097981

Printed in the United States of America
Bloomington, Indiana

This book is printed on acid-free paper.

DEDICATED TO:

WILLIAM "BILL" ERGLE

AND

EUGENE "GENE" HOLT

TABLE OF CONTENTS

FORWARD

This handbook is intended to be a guide for beginning beadworkers and should not be considered an exhaustive or authoritative treatment of the subject. I will mention some generalizations on color and style, and will introduce only the basic techniques of sewn beadwork. It is hoped that this material will guide the reader through some initial projects and prompt further study of the art of beadwork and more ambitious works of art.

There is much to be said for thorough research and authenticity. However, try not to let your quest for historical accuracy inhibit your creative process. When I first became interested in beadwork, I worried that I should emulate a single, specific aboriginal style. Finally, a very dear friend told me to "Just start putting beads on leather!" This is sound advice, and

I pass it on to the reader. As your experience grows and your abilities improve, you will become quite knowledgeable about the traditional beadwork colors and styles which are unique to the various Native American groups.

The novice beadworker should be aware that the decorative arts, other than the painting of personal events or deeds, were the exclusive domain of the women in Native American culture. Hence, no disrespect should be inferred from the use of the masculine gender in generic terms. The term "craftsman," for example, is intended to refer to anyone, male or female, that engages in the art of beadwork. Likewise, no disrespect is intended by the use of the terms "Indian" or "Tribe." Our society has become accustomed to these expressions, and in some cases, their use may make the text more discernable for the novice beadworker.

A SHORT HISTORY OF BEADS AND BEADWORK

The evolution of traditional Native American beadwork can be traced back to the ancient craft of quillwork. Early Native American craftsmen decorated personal items by embroidering them with porcupine quills colored with natural dyes. Quillwork, in turn, is an extension of painted designs. Because quillwork is a uniquely American craft, it is easy to see how the application of beads to personal articles attained such a high level of artistic expression, ability, and excellence.[1] Of all the garments, for example, that are recognizable as unique to a particular cultural or ethnic group, none are more striking than a Plains Indian "Warshirt."

Almost every culture in history has used beads for decorative and spiritual purposes, as well as to denote social status and wealth. Beads were fashioned from a variety of natural sources including bone, shell, stone, wood, and metal. Early Archaic craftsmen of the American southeast, for example, fashioned intricately designed beads depicting animals and spiritual beings from stone. Creating these miniature works of art with the tools available at the time was a laborious process and indicates that these beads were highly prized objects.[2]

Beads served some of the same functions among "civilized" European society as well. Beads were used in contemporary fashion jewelry which was exclusive to the wealthy upper classes. Additionally, the term "bead" has its origins in medieval Europe and stems from the word "bene," which means prayer.[3] The word itself, then, refers to the spiritual use of beads in rosaries during an era dominated by Christian doctrine and beliefs.

European explorers in the New World recognized early on the importance of beads in Native American culture, and elaborate trading practices arose between the native people and the newcomers. The explorers knew from their experiences in Africa that aboriginal people had a fascination for European technology and manufactured goods-especially brightly colored glass beads.[4] European beads quickly became the preferred medium of exchange in North America and were traded for food, furs, friendship, and land.

In the eastern regions of the new world, trade beads, as they came to be called, became available with Christopher Columbus' voyages of exploration during the late 15th century. In the northwest part of North America, beads came with Russian traders substantially later, probably in the late 17th or early 18th centuries.[5] As traders and trappers penetrated the frontier of the New World, they furthered the use of beads for barter. Native American groups in the central and northern parts of the continent, then, were the last to acquire beads, and among the first to acquire small beads that could be sewn onto leather. This is one reason, perhaps, that Northern Plains beadwork is considered some of the finest work of its kind.

The first beads which Native Americans acquired from European traders included a variety of large, glass beads, usually ¼" in diameter or larger, collectively termed "trade beads." However, these large beads were useful only for stringing applications. The earliest beads which could be used to emulate the visual effect of quillwork closely resembled those that we call "pony" or "E" beads and were about 1/8" in size. Most early beadwork was done using these relatively large beads. Many times, pony beads were used to create a border around quillwork designs. Over time, beads became smaller and more colorful, and the art of beadwork progressed comparably.

BEADS, NEEDLES, AND THREAD

The beads with which we are most familiar when discussing traditional Native American beadwork are commonly called "seed" beads. These tiny beads, however, did not become widely available in North America until the latter half of the 19th century; although examples do exist which date from as early as 1835.[6]

Seed beads are available today in a variety of traditional as well as contemporary colors and come in sizes ranging from size 8/o "ochos" to extremely fine size 14/o, 15/o, and even 16/o beads. When choosing beads, remember that the higher the number, the smaller the bead. The beginning beadworker should opt for size 10/o beads as these are the easiest to work with in traditional applications. Most experienced craftsmen with whom I have come into contact use size 11/o or 12/o beads. I have seen work done with size 14/o and 15/o beads and I am amazed at the intricacy of the designs as well as the ability of the craftsman and his/her eyesight.

Historically, seed beads were manufactured in Italy, Germany, Japan, and the Balkan States and beads are still available from many of the same sources. The beginning beadworker should be aware that seed beads are not perfectly uniform in shape, size, or color. Sizes differed, and continue to vary according to manufacturer. A Czech size 11/o bead, for example, is roughly the same size as a Japanese 12/o and an Italian 3/o bead. Colors will also vary slightly from one dye lot to the next even from the same manufacturer. For this reason, it is important to purchase enough beads to complete a project with a few left over for repairs. Today, the most uniform and desirable beads for traditional beadwork come from the Czech Republic.

Needle sizes follow the same rule as do seed beads: The higher the number, the smaller the diameter of the needle. You should choose a needle that is one or two sizes smaller than your beads because it may be necessary to go through a bead a number of times depending on the technique and design you are using. When using size 10/o beads, for example, I have found it advantageous to use a #11 or #12 needle.

By far, the best needles that I have found for doing traditional sewn beadwork are English Sharpes manufactured by John James & Sons of Warwickshire, England. These are available from most bead craft suppliers but can be difficult to find at local craft or sewing stores. In a pinch, a #11 or #12 Quilting needle will work. The long needles that we find labeled "beading" needles are for loom work and stringing and will not work for sewn beadwork.

Likewise, you should be conscious of the type of thread you choose to work with. Many experienced beadworkers prefer to use nylon *Nymo* thread because it is extremely strong and thin enough to pass through size 12/o and 13/o beads. However, nylon stretches and the craftsman must ensure that each stitch is tightened uniformly. I have found that regular polyester/cotton sewing thread is much easier to work with when using size 10/0 or

11/0 beads; without a substantial sacrifice in strength. Whichever type of thread you choose, be sure to wax it by pulling it over a cake of pure beeswax several times. The beeswax provides a thin protective coating and helps to eliminate tangling.

In addition to beads, needles, and thread you will also want to include in your beadwork kit a sharp pair of scissors for cutting both leather and thread, a small pair of needle-nose pliers for breaking off offensive beads, an ultra-thin needle threader, and a rubber "needle-grabber" available from quilting shops.

My Beadwork Kit:

Variety of 10/o and 11/o beads	X-Acto knife
No. 11 Sharpes needles	Six inch ruler
Dual duty poly/cotton thread	Leather thimble
Large scissors	Beeswax
Very sharp awl	Glovers needles
Needle nose pliers	Emery cloth
Small embroidery scissors	Rotary cutter
Ultra thin needle threaders	
Quilter's four-inch square layout tool	

In some of the beadwork techniques to be described, you will use a single strand of thread because you may have to pass through the beads several times. This is the case in the running stitch and with bead wrapping. In other techniques, notably the lazy stitch method, you will double the thread over in order to fill up the hole and keep the beads tight and even.

Native American artists used thin strips of sinew, or tendon material, and a sharp awl as their primary beading tools prior to European contact. A steel needle, once acquired, was considered a prized possession by Native American women and was well taken care of. Today we enjoy the benefits that modern technology and manufacturing offer, however the techniques and philosophy of beadwork remain the same.

BEADWORK SURFACES

Unquestionably, the best surface upon which to do sewn beadwork is "brain-tanned" buckskin. The term is, however, somewhat misleading because the word "tan" is derived from the use of tannic acid which is extracted from the bark of oak trees.[7] Many refer to the process of brain tanning as the "Indian method," and the Native Americans believe that every animal has enough brains to cure its own hide.

The process of making brain-tanned buckskin is the subject of another volume. However, it is important to have an understanding of what makes buckskin unique. The brain material contains, for lack of a better term, enzymes which dissolve and extract the natural glue which binds the fibers of the skin together.[8]

These fibers are further loosened and separated during the "breaking" process.

The brain-tanning method, then, *removes* substances from the hide resulting in a very light, supple; yet extremely strong leather. Inasmuch as nothing is added to the hide, the Indian method is actually a curing process. Conversely, modern tanning processes *add* chemicals to the skin which produces a heavier, thicker final product which is much more difficult to sew through.

Because the brain-tanning process is a slow and arduous task, most beginners will not have access to buckskin. When choosing commercially available leather, select one that is suede on both sides. Most commercially available deer skin is suede on one side only. The smooth side, or hair side, is the epidermal layer of tissue. This is the result of the hair being "slipped" off leaving the top layer of skin intact, rather than being scraped off as the Native Americans preferred.

There are several options available for beginners which are both appropriate and attainable. A medium weight split cowhide in a natural color is fine for larger projects. Commercial elk skin comes close to the appearance and texture of buckskin but is much heavier. Nevertheless, white elk skin makes beautiful garments which emphasizes the contrast of the beaded designs. "German-tanned" deer skin is available from several suppliers and closely mimics the properties of buckskin. Commercially available chamois, made from goat skin, is a good leather for small pouches and trim, and can be found in any automotive or department store. Try to choose a chamois that is quite thick as it is typically a very light leather and will not support the weight of a large number of beads.

With care and a sharp needle, beadwork can be done on leather that is quite heavy. There are a number of specimens, for example, of knife sheaths made from the smooth uppers of U.S. Cavalry boots. Beadwork was also applied to trade cloth, canvas, and trade blankets.

TECHNIQUES

The majority of existing beaded art as well as contemporary traditional beadwork is created using one or a combination of the following basic techniques: *Lazy stitch* or *lane stitch, running stitch, two needle appliqué stitch* or *spot stitch, bead wrapping,* and *rolled edge beading.* I have briefly described the *Crow stitch* because of its widespread use among the nations of the northern plains.

Lazy Stitch

The term *Lazy Stitch* was first coined by William C. Orchard in his 1929 treatise on Native American art styles, and was later derogatorily changed to the "Lazy Squaw Stitch" by hobbyist Ben Hunt in the 1950's.[9] Sometimes this technique is referred to as the *lane stitch* because of its finished appearance. The lazy

stitch technique involves laying down parallel rows, or lanes,

of beads and is most associated with the Sioux style of blocked,

geometric designs.

As with any beading technique, it is helpful to draw out the

plans for the design on special beadwork layout paper or on graph

paper with squares roughly equivalent to the size of the beads.

Additionally, I have found it helpful to draw out the lanes or rows

on the beadwork surface as well.

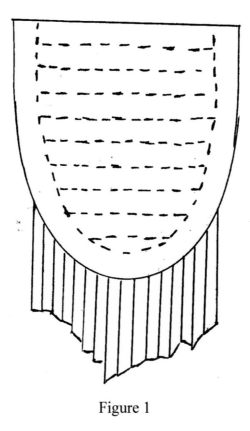

Figure 1

For most patterns, about 3/8 inch rows are desirable. This will require from five to nine beads per line depending on the size of the beads.

In order to simplify the instructions for this technique, I will use the term "line" to indicate a single strand of beads; and the word "row" to refer to the lane of beads created by a series of lines. To begin lazy stitch beadwork, double the thread over, wax it, and thread the needle pulling six or seven inches of thread through the needle. Insert the needle through the leather or cloth from the top so that the knot will lie under the first line of beads. Pass the needle up through the surface at the edge of the first row. With the needle, pick up enough beads to span the width of the row. Insure that the beads are tucked tightly against the surface and lay the line of beads across the row. Pass the needle through the surface immediately following the last bead in the line. Pull the stitch snug enough to slightly raise the beads in the middle but not so tight as to crease the leather or cloth.

Figure 2

In order to avoid exposed threads, the Native Americans did not stitch completely through the leather; instead, the stitch passed through only the top layer of the leather surface.

For the next line of beads, pass the needle up through the surface next to the last stitch and approximately ½ bead's width from the last line of beads. Experience and practice alone will

help you develop the ability to judge the bead width. You are now

ready to lay down the next line of beads. Be sure to refer to your

graphed design for the correct combination of bead colors within

the line. Continue to stitch in the same manner, sewing lines of

beads back-and-forth, until you reach the end of the first row.

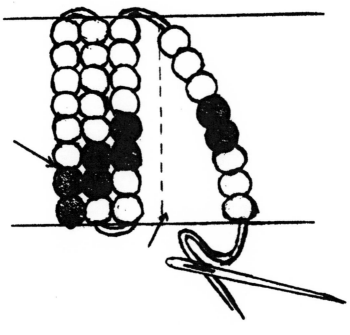

Figure 3

To begin the next row, bring the needle up right in front

of the last bead in the previous row, pick up the same number of

beads, and continue to build the row as described. Some Native groups preferred to "lock-in" the stitches by passing the needle

through the surface at a slight angle so that it comes out *behind* the

stitches in the previous row.

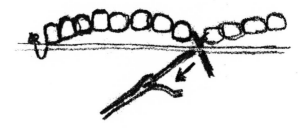

Figure 4

Locking in the stitches in this manner produces a tighter

finished appearance. Conversely , some tribes preferred a loose

appearance with visible strips of leather between the rows of beads.

Both methods are quite acceptable and visually appealing.

You will find that the lazy stitch technique produces very

visible ridges or "hills" of beads with "valleys" between the

rows. This hill and valley appearance is not at all an unpleasant

effect. Some tribes would in fact add a bead to the line in order

to make the hill more prominent, other tribes preferred a flatter appearance. It will take quite a bit of practice to perfect the lazy stitch technique and beginning beadworkers should not critique their work too harshly. Close examination of original examples will indicate that Native work was not perfect either. In fact, it is said that only Mother Earth can create anything perfect.

Running Stitch

In contrast to the "hill and valley" appearance of lazy stitch beadwork, the running stitch produces a very flat finished work. This style of beadwork is most associated with fill-in work on Eastern Woodland floral motifs and Crow style beadwork.

As with any style of beadwork, begin by drawing out the design on bead graph paper. For this technique, you will also need to outline the design on the bead surface.

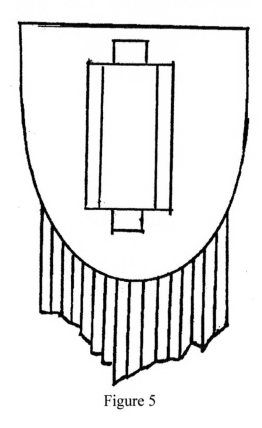

Figure 5

If the piece is to be completely covered with beadwork, you will not need to be concerned about your drawn design being visible in the finished work. However, if the piece is to be only partially beaded, be careful that the design will be covered with beads. Some experienced artisans draw the design on the back of the surface or on a piece of paper that is attached to the back.

To begin the running stitch, use a single strand of waxed thread, insert the needle through the surface along the line upon which the first row of beads will lie. Again, the knot will be

covered by the beads. Bring the needle up through the surface

at the point where the first row of beads will begin. Pick up

the desired number, I like seven or eight at a time, and color

combination of beads; remember to refer to your graphed design,

and tuck them closely against the surface. Lay the beads down

along the line, keeping them tight, and insert the needle through

the surface immediately after the last bead. Next, try to pass the

needle up through the surface between the third and fourth or

fourth and fifth bead.

Then pass the needle through the remaining beads.

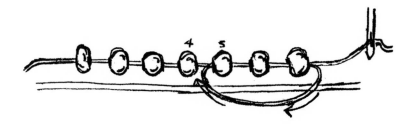

Figure 6

You are now ready to pick up more beads and complete

the next stitch. Continue in the same manner until you reach the

end of the first row of beads. In this way, it will appear as if there is a continual line of beads with no break in-between. To begin

the second row of beads, bring the needle up next to and about

½ bead's width from the last bead. Continue the technique as

described above, referring to your design graph and drawn pattern

for color combinations.

When using the running stitch, you may find that you will

sometimes need a particularly thick or thin bead in order for your

design to line up properly. This is especially the case when doing

the triangular designs that are so popular with Crow beadworkers.

Take the time to find just the right bead and your patience will be

rewarded in the quality of the finished work.

Spot Stitch

The spot stitch is used to sew down single lines of beads

in curvilinear designs. This technique is most associated with the

floral designs of the Eastern Woodland Indians. The spot stitch

is used, for example, to bead vines and to outline the flowers of

woodland designs.

The spot stitch technique requires two needles and thread. One thread will hold the beads, passing through the surface only at the beginning and end of each line of beads. The other needle is used to stitch down the line of beads every second or third bead.

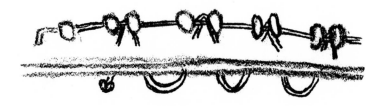

Figure 7

Once the outline of the design is completed using the spot stitch, the design is filled in using the running stitch technique as described above.

Front of the author's Crow style war-shirt. 1998

Balmoral bonnet with eastern floral beadwork motifs

James Byrne

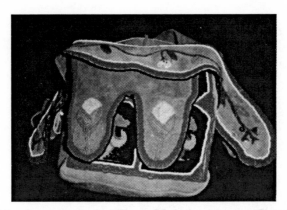

Possibles bag made by Gene Holt in eastern floral style

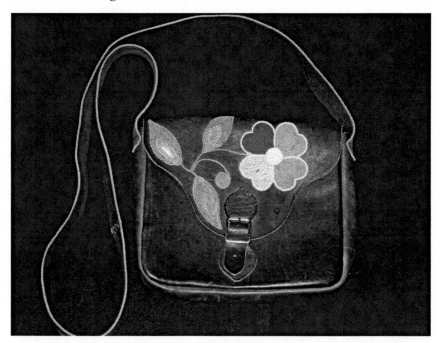

**Shooting pouch with eastern floral beadwork made by author.
1997**

Strike-a-light bag made by author 1998

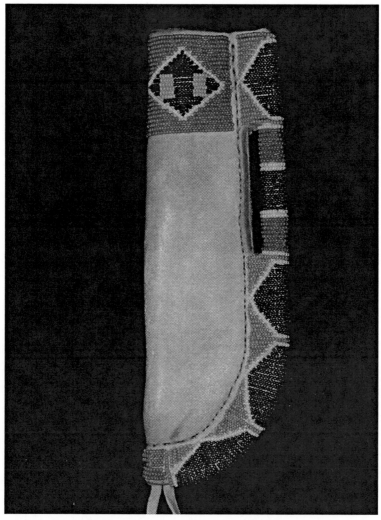

knife sheath made by author with rolled edge beadwork. 2002

James Byrne

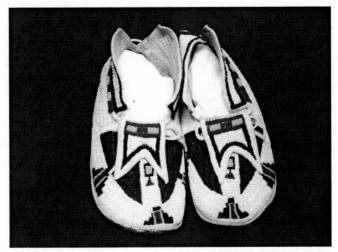

Fully beaded moccasins made by Gene Holt in Sioux style 1996

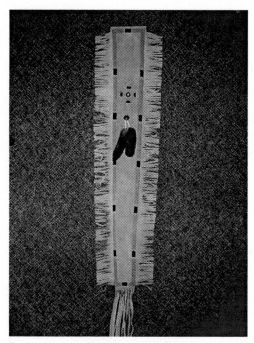

Large flute bag

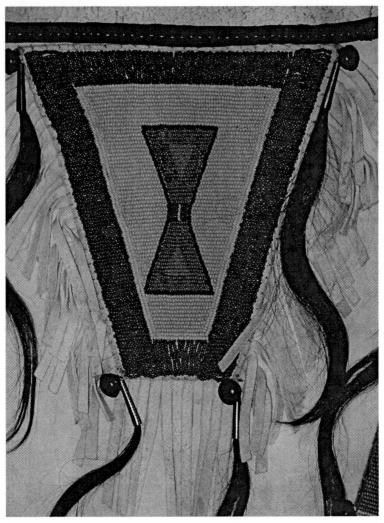

Chest piece of author's beaded shirt in classic Crow design

Detail of beaded strip on sleve of author's Crow style shirt

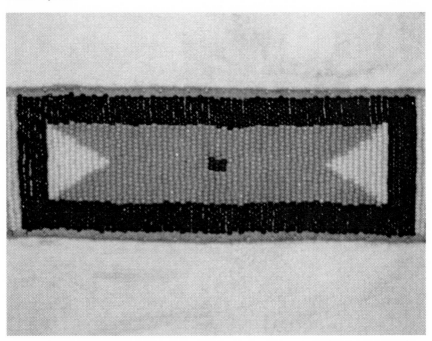

Detail of beaded design elements on author's Plains style shirt
(a)

Detail of beaded design elements on author's Plains style shirt
(b)

Back of the author's Crow style shirt

Detail of back of author's Plains Indian style shirt

Detail of beaded cones over mink pelt

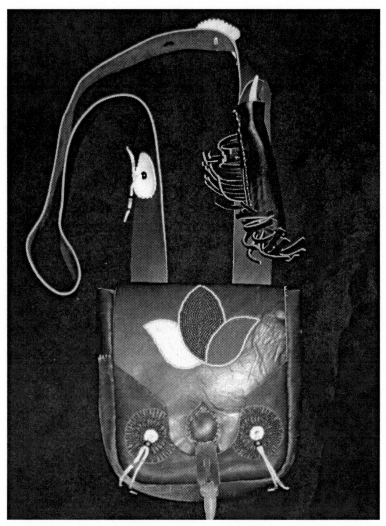

Eastern style shooting pouch made by author. 1998

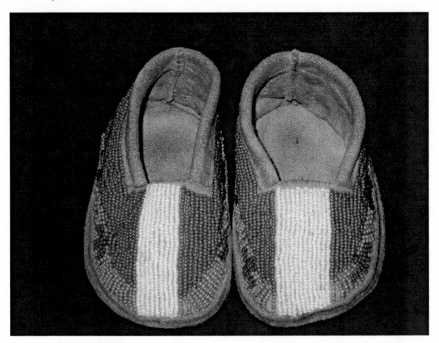

Child's moccasins made by author. 1995

Crow style possibles bag made by author. 1999

Sioux style war-shirt made by Bill Ergle. 1994

Crow Stitch

The Crow stitch is so-called because of its' preference among Crow women. However, the term is somewhat of a misnomer as this technique was popular among other Northern Plains Tribes as well. The Crow stitch is sometimes referred to as a modified Lazy stitch because it combines elements of the lazy stitch and spot stitch techniques. This stitch produces a very flat, very neat finished appearance.

The Crow stitch utilizes several steps. First, the outline of the design is done using the spot stitch. Once the outline is completed, the design is filled in using long lines of beads. This is why it is called a modified lazy stitch; the design is created with the same back-and-forth rhythm of the lazy stitch using substantially more beads. Once the design had been created, a third needle and thread is used to stitch down every second or third bead in each line of beads.

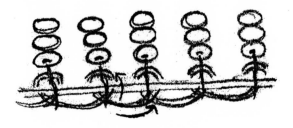

Figure 8

Because you will only be passing the needle through the beads once, you will use a double strand of waxed thread to build the design. Again, we begin with the knot on top of the bead surface. Then pass the needle through the surface at the point where the first line of beads will begin. Pick up enough beads, in the correct color combination, to span the length of the design and pass the needle through the surface at the last bead. For the next stitch pass the needle up through the surface next to and ½ bead's width from the previous line of beads and continue to build the design in this manner.

Once the beaded design is filled in, prepare another needle and thread and backstitch each line of beads working perpendicular to the design until you reach the bottom of the beadwork. Move the needle two or three beads over and repeat the process. In this way, each line of beads is fastened down every ¼ inch or so to create the desired flat appearance.

The Crow stitch takes quite a bit of practice to master, and is best for beading large, flat articles such as blanket strips. Crow Beadwork often had bead outlines going in different directions: The design element, a rectangle for example, was outlined with beads going both horizontally and vertically on the beadwork surface. Once the design was outlined, often with white or dark blue beads, the Crow stitch was used to create the background and fill-in the design.

Bead Wrapping

To wrap beads around a round object such as a fan or rattle handle, pipe stem, or feather quills, you will need to use a modified version of the running stitch described earlier. The object to be beaded must first be covered with buckskin or other leather in order to provide a surface upon which to bead.

When the wrapping method is employed, the return stitch of the running technique will likely not pass completely through the beadwork surface. Rather, the thread will lie under only the surface of the leather. For this reason, you will need to use substantially less beads than in the running stitch. Sometimes there is only room for two or three beads on smaller objects.

Begin the wrapping technique with a single strand of thread. Again, pass the needle through the top of the surface so that the knot will be covered with beads. In this case, because there is a solid object under the beadwork surface, you will need to pass the needle backwards through the surface at an angle along an imaginary line upon which the beads will lie.

When the needle comes to the surface, pick up the desired number and colors of beads and lay them along the same imaginary line. Make sure that the beads are tucked tightly against the thread and surface. Insert the needle immediately following the last bead and, again angle the needle backward so that it comes out approximately in the middle of the line of beads. Recall that you may be using only a few beads in this case. Pass the needle through the remaining beads and make the next stitch in the same

manner.

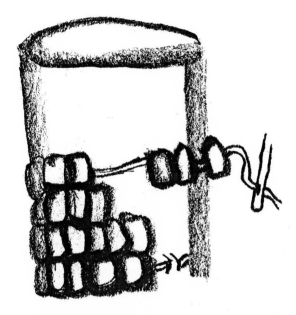

Figure 9

When the row of beads has completely encircled the object,

pass the needle through the first couple of beads that you stitched

down. Bring the needle out next to the previous row and begin

to stitch as described. By passing the needle through the first

few beads of the previous row, you will straighten the obviously

crooked bead that resulted from the shift in rows.

Edge Beading

Edge beading is an important final step to many beadwork projects and is sometimes the single greatest element of beadwork on an article. Although there are many styles of edge beading, most are contemporary in origin. The most common method of edge beading in traditional beadwork is the simple rolled edge technique. Rolled edge beadwork is most often seen on the tops of open bags, such as pipe bags, and around the seams of bags and pouches.

In the rolled edge method, the beads create a solid beaded border completely around the edge or seam of the article. Begin by passing the needle through the surface two or three beads width from the edge. Pick up enough beads to wrap over the edge and reach down the side the same distance as the first side.

Figure 10

Stitch completely through the surface so that the needle emerges in line with and ½ bead's width from the first row of beads. Continue in the same manner until the edge is completely covered.

Seam Beading

The seams of pouches and bags may be covered using the rolled edge technique described above. In some cases however, you may wish to bead over a flat seam. This is the case where the uppers of a pair of moccasins are sewn together in the back. On a pair of fully beaded moccasins, you will surely want to cover the seam so that the entire surface is covered with beads.

To begin this technique, secure the thread by passing the needle through the surface under the first row of sewn beadwork on one side of the article, so that the knot is covered. Pass the needle back through the surface two or three beads back on the first row of sewn beads. Pass the needle through the last few beads of that row and pick up enough beads to cover the seam and reach the opposing row of beads on the other side of the sewn beadwork.

Now pass the needle through the first two or three beads of that row. Bring the needle out and pass it through the first few beads of the next row, pick up enough beads to reach the opposite row and pass the needle through the first two or three beads of that row.

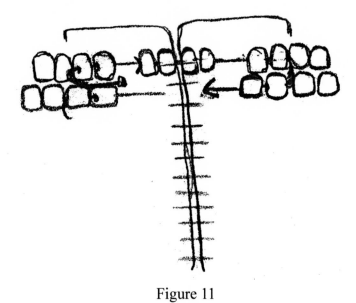

Figure 11

Continue in the same manner, working back-and-forth through the second or third bead of each row until the seam is covered. In this way, it will appear that the row of beads passes completely around the article with no breaks. Note that the thread passes through the beads only and is secured to the surface only at the top and bottom of the seam.

Loomwork

I will mention loom work only briefly because most traditional beadwork is sewn directly onto a surface using one of the techniques described above. The use of loomed beadwork was limited almost exclusively to a few tribes of the northeast and great lakes regions. Loom work enjoys a degree of popularity today as a result of the writings of hobbyists and the availability of inexpensive craft kits using looms. The most notable examples of true loom work are the bandolier bags created by Ojibwa craftsmen. It should be noted that the inexpensive, machine made loom work available today cannot match the skill or intricate designs of the native artisans.

Tying Off

In most of the techniques that I have described, we will tie off the thread using the following method. To tie off the thread after the last stitch, make sure the needle is on the bottom side of the beaded surface. Pull the stitch tight and insert the needle through just the top layer of leather right next to the thread-don't pull the needle all the way through. Wrap the thread around the

needle shaft two or three times. Now pull the needle through while

holding the knot. When the knot is against the surface, give the

thread a little tug and cut it off about 1/8 inch from the knot.

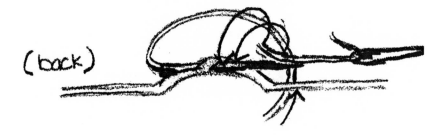

(back)

Figure 12

THE USE OF COLOR

There are generally two schools of thought when discussing the use of color in Native American beadwork. The first holds that each color had a symbolic and exclusive meaning. The other argues that while certain bead colors were preferred by some tribes over others, the symbolism, if any, was a subjective and very personal matter. However, through tradition or custom, some generalizations can be made on color representation.

One interpretation on the use of color associates colors with the four root elements of life: Earth, wind, fire, and water. Among the Sioux, the color red is associated with the earth; wind or air is identified with the colors green or blue; fire is represented by the color yellow; and water corresponds to the color white. The Sioux also used red to represent strength and war while white illustrated peace.[10]

Among the Crow Indians, whose beadwork is regarded as some of the most striking, color and design symbolism was interpreted in more militant terms. The Crow associated the color red with property, blood, or the desire for revenge. Black, although rarely employed, was used to signify the clouds or realized revenge. White represented purity, hail, or fog. Finally, green was used to depict the earth.[11]

Another popular interpretation of color symbolism assigns the dominant colors to the four cardinal directions or winds. The Sioux, for example, assigned the color red to the East, yellow to the South, black to the West, and white to the North. Among the Cherokee Indians of the southeast, the color red represented the East, white the South, black the West, and blue the North. The Pawnee Indians' use of color shows even further variance on directional symbolism: The color black was assigned to the Northeast; red to the Southeast; white to the Southwest; and yellow to the Northwest.[12]

Obviously there are considerable variations on the use of directional symbolism. Individuals within a particular tribe may even choose to use different color combinations. For example, one may select to use a color that was revealed to him or her during a vision quest or dream.[13] This further illustrates that there were no hard and fast rules and that color symbolism was unique to the individual and a very private issue.

The widespread use of the color black illustrates a major contradiction in beaded designs. That is, while black figures prominently in directional symbolism, it is rarely used in beadwork. Instead, dark blue was almost always substituted in the place of black on beaded designs. This practice was the result of a number of influences. First, the color black is often associated with formlessness, the mysterious, and the unknown.[14] Additionally, the West is also associated, though in a lesser degree, with various hues of blue.[15] Finally, Native Americans held a particular fascination for the color blue because of the difficulty in producing a dark blue from natural dyes for use in quillwork.[16]

Because the symbolism of color is ultimately and intimate and highly individualized question, novice beadworkers should follow one basic rule of color usage, and that rule is **contrast**. The colors must be bold enough to make the designs discernable even at a distance. Native craftsmen prefer to use lighter shades as background colors in order to make the design elements more conspicuous. Hence their partiality for white or light blue beads as background colors.

The single element that separates good beadwork from exceptional beadwork is the ability to utilize color and design contrast.[17] Although those people gifted with innate artistic abilities enjoy a substantial head start, anyone can develop competence in building distinctive color and design features with experience and practice. Again, do not be overly critical of your work. Every great artist must learn their craft, and the only way to gain experience in beadwork is to do it.

The traditional beadwork colors for some of the major Plains Tribes are depicted in the following table:

Tribe	Background Colors	Design Colors
Sioux	White or Light Blue; occasionally Yellow, Cheyenne Pink, Light Green, and Medium Green	Various shades of Blue, Medium Green, Dark Green, Cheyenne Pink, and Yellow; rarely Black
Crow	Light Blue, Cheyenne Pink, and Lavender; occasionally, White and Yellow	Various shades of Blue, Red, Cheyenne Pink, Yellow, various shades of Green, and White
Cheyenne	Almost exclusively White	Turquoise Blue, Navy Blue, Medium Green, Dark Green, Cheyenne Pink, Red, and Yellow; rarely Black
Blackfoot	White or Light Blue; occasionally, Medium Blue	Black, Red, Yellow, Green, Cheyenne Pink, and Royal Blue; occasionally Medium Blue, and Orange
Comanche	White, Powder Blue, and Red; occasionally Medium Green and Cheyenne Pink	Dark Red, Powder Blue, and Royal Blue; occasionally Yellow, Light Green, and Medium Green
Ojibwa	White, Yellow, Light Blue, and Cheyenne Pink; occasionally Dark Blue, Black, Red, and Green	Virtually all shades and colors
Pawnee	White; sometimes Yellow, Light Blue and Cheyenne Pink	Red, Yellow, various shades of Blue, Cheyenne Pink, Dark Green, and Medium Green
Cherokee	No beaded background used	White, Dark Red, Yellow, Dark Green, Light Green, and Cheyenne Pink,
Shawnee	Powder Blue, Cheyenne Pink, Royal Blue, and Dark Red	White, Powder Blue, Cheyenne Pink, Dark Red, and Medium Green; sometimes Yellow

Table was created from information in Crazy Crow catalog #21

DESIGN ELEMENTS

Careful examination of traditional Native American beaded articles as a genre yields three distinct design styles which were, and are, utilized in beadwork. Women of the Eastern Woodlands Tribes exhibited a clear disposition for *floral* motifs while craftsmen of the Plains preferred **geometric** designs. The **pictographic** style was utilized throughout North America to commemorate some heroic deed, successful hunt, or other important event in the life of the wearer.

With the exception of the latter, these design elements carry no particular symbolic meaning and served only artistic roles. Often, the more common motifs acquired names through repeated use, but the meanings of the designs, if any, is highly subjective.[18]

Although one could assert that colors carry more symbolic meaning than designs, both are very personal and individual matters. It has also been argued that beaded designs served a societal function among people with no written language. That is, the chosen design elements identify the wearer and depict the significant events in his or her life. Others argue that the designs are purely aesthetic and that the symbolism resides in the beaded object or its purpose. Beadwork then is simply the "glorification or respected beautification of the object."[19] Ultimately, the symbolism of beaded designs, like that of colors, is unique to the individual wearer or maker. It would be inappropriate for us to attempt to interject our interpretations upon them.

Some of the more popular design motifs in the geometric style of the Plains Indians include triangles, crosses, stars, diamonds, the hour glass, squares and rectangles, and beaded borders. These designs, while similar, carry different names in various tribes. The stepped triangle, for example, is termed "mountain" by Blackfoot craftsmen and "tipi" in Sioux work. Another common motif is the "buffalo track" or "horse track" which looks like the imprint of the animal's hoof. This design

element is often seen on the uppers of Plains moccasins.

Other Plains geometric designs include some combination

of squares, triangle, and straight lines.[20] These basic elements are

assembled rather like quilt patterns into such designs as the Lakota

"forked tree," dragonfly," and "arrow;" and the Apache "saw

tooth."[21] Others include the Crow "morning star," "thunder," and

"lightning."[22]

Pictographic designs certainly carry specific meanings as

they are used to recall important events in the life of the wearer.

However, it is important to note that this meaning is personal and

outsiders should not attempt to apply or interpret the meaning

of these designs. Turtles, lizards, buffalo, and dragonflies are

common pictographic motifs. More elaborate designs may depict a

warrior on horseback, victory over an enemy, or a successful hunt.

The floral beadwork of the eastern tribes is perhaps a

product of their environment. The curvilinear vines, flowers, and

leaves are doubtlessly depictions or representations of the heavily

forested homelands of the Indians which stretched from the Ohio

Valley to the eastern part of present-day Texas and east from the Mississippi River. These depictions may be either very realistic depictions or quite surrealistic representations of the surrounding fauna utilizing a variety of bright colors to emphasize the myriad of colors found in nature.

As a final note on the symbolism of color and design, recall that the use of seed beads did not become widespread until the latter half of the nineteenth century. By that time, the majority of Eastern tribes and many of the Plains Indians had been removed from their homelands and forced onto reservations in the west. The cross-culturalization of various indigenous groups during the "Reservation Period" resulted in the blending of regional styles and color preferences. Additionally, particularly gifted artisans were often commissioned to do beadwork for individuals who could afford to pay for their services. Finally, we must consider that many beaded articles were produced expressly for trade with neighboring tribes and White frontiersmen. The difficulty of ascribing symbolic meanings to beaded designs becomes apparent when we consider all of these circumstances.

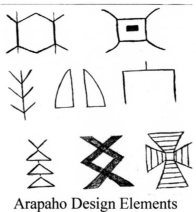

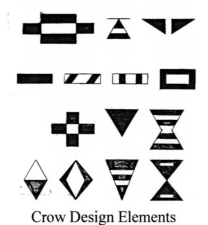

Arapaho Design Elements

Crow Design Elements

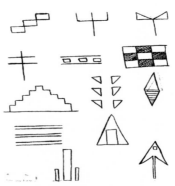

Sioux Design Elements

62

CONCLUSION

I hope that this short guide book has piqued your interest in traditional Native American beadwork. You will doubtless want to see some finished beadwork for yourself. Plan to attend a local pow-wow and observe the dancers' regalia. Be sure to ask permission before taking photographs. Certainly, visit your local library and research beaded articles to get an idea of what you want to produce. To get a closer look, visit a museum that has beaded articles on display.

Once you have chosen a project, do not critique your work too harshly; the finished article usually comes out quite nice. I have often been tempted to pull out the stitches and start over but I am usually satisfied with my finished work. A close look at genuine pieces will reveal that native beadwork is not perfect. Rather than detracting from the visual effect, the imperfections add that touch of primitive uniqueness that makes beadwork even more appealing.

Finally, take care not to chose a difficult work as your first attempt at beadwork. Practice on smaller items with simple design and color elements to perfect the techniques then move on to more ambitious projects. With this said, get your beadwork kit together and "Just start putting beads on leather!"

APPENDIX 1

Beadwork supplies and publications

Crazy Crow Trading Post
P.O. Box 847
Pottsboro, Texas 75076-0847

The Leather Factory
3101 Williams Street
P.O. Box 2430
Chattanooga, Tennessee 37409

Eagle Feather Trading Post
168 West 12th Street
Ogden, Utah 84404

Shipwreck Beads
2727 Westmoor Court SW
Olympia, Washington 98502

Leather Unlimited
7155 Highway B
P.O. Box L
Belgium, Wisconsin 53004-0905

Grey Owl Indian Craft Sales Corp.
132-05 Merrick Blvd.
Jamaica, New York 11434

Wakeda Trading Post
P.O. Box 19146
Sacramento, California 95819

Western Trading Post
P.O. Box 9070 W
Denver, Colorado 80209-0070

Bovis Bead Company
P.O. Box 111
Bisbee, Arizona 85603

APPENDIX 2

Beadwork Graph Paper

NOTES

Joel Monture, *The Complete Guide to Traditional Native American Beadwork* (New York: Macmillan Publishing Co., 1992) p. 2.

[2] Susan C. Power, "Archaic Effigy Beads in the Native American Southeast," *Ornament* 23 (Winter 1999): 54-55.

[3] Mark M. Johnson, "Pure Vision: American Bead Artists," *Arts & Activities,* 120 (December 1996): 33.

[4] David Dean, *Beading in the Native American Tradition* (Loveland: Interweave Press, 2002) p.3.

[5] Kate C. Duncan, *Northern Athapascan Art: A Beadwork tradition* (Seattle, University of Washington Press, 1989) p. 41.

[6] Monte Smith, *The Technique of North American Indian Beadwork* (Odgen: Eagle's View Publishing, 1983) p. 74.

[7] William A. Ergle and Eugene Holt, *Over the Hill Buckskin* (Rome: The Franklin Press, 1995) p. 6.

[8] *Ibid.*

[9] Monture, p. 36.

[10] Frederick Webb Hodge, *Handbook of the American Indians North of Mexico,* part 1 (New York: Rowman and Littlefield, 1971)

[11] William Wildschut and John C. Ewers, *Crow Indian Beadwork: A Descriptive and Historical Study* (Ogden: Eagle's View Publishing, 1985) p. 47.

[12] Kenneth Cohen, *Honoring the Medicine* (New York: Ballantine Books, 2003) p. 53.

[13] *Ibid.*

[14] Kenneth Meadows, *The Medicine Way* (Shaftsbury: Element, 1990) p. 120.

[15] Examine the medicine wheel chart on page 69 of Kenneth Meadows' *Earth medicine* (Shaftsbury: Element, 1996).

[16] Dean, pp. 4-5.

[17] Monture, p. 72.

[18] Robert E. Spencer and Jesse D. Jennings *et al, The Native Americans* 2nd edition (New York: Harper and Row, 1977) p. 337.

[19] Monture, p. 73.

[20] Spencer and Jennings *et al*. p. 337

[21] Wildschut and Ewers, pp. 44-45.

[22] Monture, p. 73.

BIBLIOGRAPHY

Kenneth Cohen, *Honoring the Medicine* (New York: Ballantine
Books, 2003) p. 53.

David Dean, *Beading in the Native American Tradition* (Loveland:
Interweave Press, 2002) p.3.

Kate C. Duncan, *Northern Athapascan Art: A Beadwork tradition*
(Seattle, University of Washington Press, 1989) p. 41.

Ergle, William and Holt, Eugene. *Over the Hill Buckskin.* Rome:
The Franklin Press, 1995.

Hodge, Frederick Webb, ed. *Handbook of the American Indians
North of Mexico.* Vol. 1. New York: Rowman and
Littlefield, 1971.

Johnson, Mark M. "Pure Vision: American Bead Artists," *Arts &
Activities,* 120 (December 1996): 33-35.

Meadows, Kenneth. *The Medicine Way.* Shaftsbury: Element.

    1990.

Monture, Joel. *The Complete Guide to Traditional Native*

    American Beadwork. New York: Macmillan. 1993.

Power, Susan C. "Archaic Effigy Beads in the Native American

    Southeast." *Ornament.* Vol. 23. (Winter 1999): 54-57.

Smith, Monte. *The Technique of North American Indian*

    Beadwork. Odgen: Eagle's View Publishing. 1983.

Spencer, Robert E. and Jennings, Jesse D. *et al. The Native*

    Americans. 2nd edition. New York: Harper and Row. 1977.

Wildschut, William and Ewers, John C. *Crow Indian Beadwork:*

    A Descriptive and Historical Study. Ogden: Eagle's View

    Publishing. 1985.

ABOUT THE AUTHOR

James J. Byrne holds a Bachelor of Arts in History from Berry College in Rome, Georgia. His interest in Native American culture began at an early age as a member of the Boy Scouts m Northwest Georgia; an area rich in Native American History. His mentor and former Scoutmaster later taught him the basics of beadwork and buck skinning. Mr. Byrne continues to work actively with the scouting movement which inspired him to compile this handbook. He works for the public library system and lives in Kingston, Georgia with his three children.

CPSIA information can be obtained at www.ICGtesting.com
Printed in the USA
BVOW021048190112

280944BV00002B/192/A